COMPLETE GUIDE TO ZEBU FARMING

Optimal Breeding, Nutritional Management, Health Care, Marketing Strategies, And Sustainable Practices For Profitable Livestock Production

GIOVANNI MALAKAI

© [2024] [Giovanni Malakai]. All rights reserved.

Except for brief quotations included in critical reviews and certain other noncommercial uses allowed by copyright law, no part of this publication may be reproduced, distributed, or transmitted in any form or by any means, including photocopying, recording, or other electronic or mechanical methods, without the publisher's prior written permission. Write to the publisher at the address below, addressing your letter to the "Attention: Permissions Coordinator," requesting permission.

DISCLAIMER

This book's content is solely intended for informational and educational purposes. The author and publisher of this book make no express or implied representations or warranties of any kind regarding the completeness, accuracy, reliability, suitability, or availability of the information, products, services, or related graphics contained in it, even though every effort has been made to ensure their accuracy and dependability. You consequently absolutely assume all risk associated with any reliance you may have on such material.

The author's own experiences and studies serve as the foundation for the techniques and procedures covered in this book. They might not be appropriate for every circumstance or person. Before putting any advice or recommendations from this book into practice, readers should use their own discretion and take into account their unique situation. Consulting with qualified professionals who specialize in veterinary care and animal management is always a good idea. Any direct, indirect, incidental or consequential damages resulting from using or relying on the material in this book are disclaimed by the author and publisher. Any decisions made by the reader based on the information presented herein are at their own risk.

TABLE OF CONTENTS

- CHAPTER ONE 13
  - INTRODUCTION TO ZEBU FARMING 13
    - WHAT IS FARMING IN ZEBU? 13
    - ZEBU FARMING: WHY OPT FOR IT? 14
    - KNOWLEDGE OF ZEBU BREEDS 15
    - CRUCIAL TOOLS FOR ZEBU FARMING 17
    - ORGANIZING YOUR ZEBU FARM 18
- CHAPTER TWO 21
  - STARTING A ZEBU FARMING BUSINESS 21
    - CHOOSING THE CORRECT ZEBU BREED 21
    - PUTTING UP APPROPRIATE FACILITIES AND HOUSING 22
    - KNOWING ZEBU FEEDING AND NUTRITION 23
    - ZEBU'S HEALTH AND CARE MANAGEMENT 25
    - ZEBU BREEDING METHODS 26
- CHAPTER THREE 29
  - ZEBU FARMING METHODS 29
    - ACTIVITIES AND DAILY SCHEDULES ON A ZEBU FARM 29
    - SEASONAL UPKEEP AND CARE 30
    - TAKING CARE OF ZEBU PASTURES AND GRAZING 32
    - ECOLOGICAL METHODS IN ZEBU AGRICULTURE 33
    - MAINTAINING DOCUMENTS AND MANAGING DATA 34
- CHAPTER FOUR 37
  - ZEBU VETERINARY AND HEALTH SERVICES 37
    - COMMON HEALTH PROBLEMS AND SYMPTOMS IN ZEBU ... 37

- IMMUNIZATION AND HEALTH PREVENTION 39
- CONTROL OF PARASITES IN ZEBU 41
- HANDLING EMERGENCIES AND INJURIES 43

CHAPTER FIVE 45
BREEDING AND REPRODUCTION OF ZEBU 45
- RECOGNIZING THE REPRODUCTIVE CYCLES OF ZEBU 45
- BREEDING PROCEDURES AND STRATEGIES 46
- PREGNANCY MANAGEMENT AND CARE 47
- ZEBU CALVES' BIRTH AND NEONATAL CARE 48
- STRATEGIES FOR GENETIC IMPROVEMENT 49

CHAPTER SIX 51
ZEBU MANAGEMENT AND PRODUCTION 51
- PRODUCTION OF MILK AND MANAGEMENT OF DAIRIES 51
- MEAT PROCESSING AND QUALITY CONTROL 52
- HARVESTING WOOL AND FIBER FROM ZEBU 53
- VALUE-ENHANCED ZEBU GOODS 54
- ZEBU FARMING'S MARKETING AND SALES STRATEGIES 56

CHAPTER SEVEN 57
ENVIRONMENTAL FACTORS IN ZEBU AGRICULTURE 57
- ECOLOGICAL FARMING METHODS 57
- POLLUTION CONTROL AND WASTE MANAGEMENT 58
- PRESERVATION OF NATURAL RESOURCES 59
- CLIMATE MODIFICATION FOR ZEBU AGRICULTURE 60
- SOCIAL RESPONSIBILITY AND COMMUNITY INVOLVEMENT 61

CHAPTER EIGHT 63

- REGULATORY AND LEGAL ASPECTS 63
  - RECOGNIZING THE REGULATIONS FOR ZEBU FARMING 63
  - ZEBU FARMS' LICENSES & PERMITS 64
  - OBSERVANCE OF LAWS CONCERNING ANIMAL WELFARE 65
  - FINANCIAL REPORTING AND TAXATION 66
  - ZEBU FARMS' INSURANCE 67
- CHAPTER NINE 69
  - TYPICAL WORRIES IN ZEBU FARMING 69
    - HANDLING PREDATORS OF ZEBU TYPE 69
    - MANAGING ZEBU'S AGGRESSIVE BEHAVIOR 70
    - CONTROLLING DISEASE OUTBREAKS 71
    - WEATHER AND DROUGHT ISSUES 72
    - SUSTAINING SAFETY AND SECURITY ON FARMS 73
- CHAPTER TEN 75
  - FAQS ABOUT ZEBU FARMING 75
    - HOW LONG DOES A ZEBU LIVE? 75
    - WHAT IS THE REQUIRED AREA FOR A ZEBU FARM? 76
    - WHAT DISTINGUISHES ZEBU CATTLE FROM OTHER KINDS OF ... 77
    - CAN ZEBU LIVE IN A VARIETY OF CLIMATES? 79
    - WHEN COMPARING ZEBU FARMING TO OTHER LIVESTOCK, HOW ... 80
- CHAPTER ELEVEN 83
  - SOURCES & ADDITIONAL READING 83
    - SUGGESTED READINGS AND SOURCES 83
    - ZEBU FARMERS' ONLINE COMMUNITIES AND FORUMS 84
    - WORKSHOPS AND TRAINING PROGRAMS 86

ORGANIZATIONS, BOTH GOVERNMENTAL AND NON-GOVERNMENTAL, IN ZEBU FARMING 87

WEBSITES AND TOOLS THAT ARE HELPFUL FOR ZEBU FARM 88

ABOUT THE BOOK

For anyone looking to get started in Zebu farming or improve their current skills and knowledge, the "Complete Guide to Zebu Farming" is an invaluable resource. Zebu farming stands out in the agricultural scene because of its many benefits and is known for its resilience and versatility. This book delves deeply into the nuances of Zebu farming, covering everything from grasping basic principles to mastering sophisticated methods and negotiating regulatory environments.

This guide's main focus is on Zebu breeds, highlighting their distinctive qualities and the advantages they offer farming enterprises. After that, it explores the fundamental gear needed for Zebu farming, making sure that readers have the resources they need to maximize their output and effectiveness.

One of the most important parts of this book, which acts as an introduction for newcomers by explaining important topics including choosing the best Zebu breed, setting up suitable housing and amenities, and understanding Zebu's diet and feeding needs. It also explores health and care management practices, which are critical to preserving Zebu herd health.

Going ahead, it summarizes the routine procedures and seasonal variations in Zebu farming, placing a focus on environmentally friendly approaches and efficient record-keeping techniques. In the meantime, it explores the topic of Zebu health and veterinary care, giving readers the information they need to handle common health problems, put preventative healthcare measures into practice, and handle emergencies skillfully.

The book also explores the complexities of Zebu breeding and reproduction, offering details on breeding methods, genetic improvement plans, and reproductive cycles. For those looking to improve the genetic qualities of their Zebu herds and maximize their breeding strategies, this section is helpful.

It is mostly devoted to a thorough examination of Zebu production and management, including topics like milk production, meat quality control, wool and fiber harvesting, and efficient marketing and sales tactics designed especially for Zebu goods.

It delves deeply into the environmental aspects of Zebu farming, emphasizing the importance of sustainable practices, waste management tactics, climate adaption techniques, and community engagement activities in promoting an environmentally conscious and responsible agricultural strategy.

It demystifies the legal and regulatory environment around Zebu farming, providing information on permits, taxes, animal welfare legislation, insurance, and other factors that are essential for maintaining both legal compliance and financial stability.

In addition to stressing farm security and safety precautions, it tackles frequent issues Zebu farmers confront, such as regulating aggressive behavior and dealing with predators as well as disease outbreaks and weather-related difficulties.

To provide readers with answers to frequently asked questions, it includes a thorough FAQ section that covers a wide range of topics, including lifespan, space needs, climatic adaptation, profitability comparisons, and more.

The book provides access to a variety of extra resources and reading material, such as suggested books, online discussion boards, training courses, governmental and non-governmental organizations, helpful websites, and tools designed especially for Zebu farm management.

This book endeavors to equip Zebu farmers with the necessary knowledge, tools, and tactics to prosper in the ever-changing landscape of Zebu farming, promote sustainable practices, and propel industry success through its captivating and inspiring tone.

CHAPTER ONE

INTRODUCTION TO ZEBU FARMING

WHAT IS FARMING IN ZEBU?

Raising Zebu cattle, a species native to South Asia noted for its resilience to several diseases and climate adaptation is referred to as "Zebu farming." These calves can be identified by their noticeable dewlap, drooping ears, and pronounced hump over the shoulders. Zebu farming entails several activities, including management, healthcare, feeding, and breeding, to maintain the animals' well-being and productivity.

Before beginning Zebu farming, one must be aware of the fundamental needs of these animals, which include adequate housing, wholesome food, and medical procedures. Enough room for grazing and relaxing, as well as shelter from inclement weather, should be provided by housing. To promote growth and development, feeding Zebu cattle entails providing a balanced diet of grass, hay, grains, and mineral supplements.

To enhance desired qualities including milk output, meat quality, and disease resistance, zebu farming also includes breeding initiatives.

Techniques like artificial insemination and selective breeding are frequently employed to accomplish these objectives. In addition, to keep the herd healthy and avoid illnesses, routine veterinary examinations, vaccines, and de worming are crucial.

ZEBU FARMING: WHY OPT FOR IT?

Zebu farming may be a profitable and satisfying endeavor for several reasons. First of all, Zebu cattle are hardy in tropical and subtropical climates, which is beneficial in situations where heat and humidity are prevalent. Farmers are also drawn to them because of their resistance to diseases prevalent in these regions and their capacity to flourish on roughage.

Zebu cattle are also renowned for being multipurpose animals that can produce both meat and milk. Farmers can meet various market demands and diversify their revenue streams because of this adaptability. Zebu cattle provide meat that is typically leaner and tastes different, making it desirable to people seeking out healthier protein sources.

Zebu farming can also support sustainable agricultural methods. Compared to intensive grain-fed livestock systems, these cattle have a smaller ecological footprint because they are effective at converting forages into valued products like milk and meat. Farmers may support local food systems, conserve natural resources, and advance biodiversity by implementing Zebu farming.

KNOWLEDGE OF ZEBU BREEDS

Zebu cattle come in a variety of breeds, each with distinct qualities and applicability for particular uses. Brahman, Nelore, Gir, Guzerat, and Sahiwal are some of the well-known Zebu breeds.

Farmers must have a thorough understanding of these breeds to make wise judgments about breeding plans and output targets.

For example, Brahman cattle are renowned for their versatility, heat tolerance, and disease and insect resistance. They are frequently preferred in areas with harsh weather. Nelore cattle are a good fit for meat production systems because of their reputation for high-quality meat, lean muscle growth, and effective feed conversion.

Gir cattle are highly valued due to their high milk yield, placid disposition, and capacity to flourish on substandard feeds. In addition to having high meat and milk quality, Guzerat cattle are resistant to heat stress and ticks. Sahiwal cattle are prized for their ability to withstand disease, produce a lot of milk, and adapt to a variety of situations.

Certain characteristics of each Zebu breed can be advantageous to farmers according to their production goals and the surrounding conditions.

In Zebu farming operations, producers can maximize productivity and sustainability by choosing the appropriate breed or putting crossbreeding schemes into place.

CRUCIAL TOOLS FOR ZEBU FARMING

Utilizing a variety of necessary tools and facilities is necessary for successful zebu farming to guarantee the efficiency and well-being of the herd. For the cattle to be kept within approved grazing areas and shielded from predators, an adequate fence is first and foremost essential.

Depending on the topography and available funds, high-quality fencing materials like barbed wire, electric fencing, or wooden posts should be employed.

In addition, feeding supplies such as troughs, hay racks, and water troughs are required to give the cattle a healthy diet and enough water. To minimize feed waste and provide simple access, these should be arranged strategically.

To shield cattle from harsh weather, shelter buildings like barns or sheds are necessary. They offer shade during hot weather and protection from rain or chilly winds.

Furthermore, routine chores like de worming, immunizations, and pregnancy tests depend on the proper handling of equipment like headgates, chutes, and corrals.

Designing these facilities with safety in mind will guarantee the well-being of the animals as well as the effectiveness of farm activities. Successful Zebu farming techniques depend on making quality equipment investments and keeping up with routine maintenance.

ORGANIZING YOUR ZEBU FARM

For any Zebu farming endeavor to be successful, careful preparation is essential. Whether they are concentrating on breeding programs, milk production, or meat production, farmers should first identify their aims and objectives.

Understanding customer demand, pricing patterns, and competition through market research can aid in decision-making and the creation of a workable company plan.

In addition, determining the land, water, feed, and capital investments that are available is crucial for organizing the infrastructure and farm architecture. To maximize cattle nutrition and land utilization, adequate pasture management strategies that include rotational grazing and forage supplementation should be put into practice.

Furthermore, keeping the herd healthy and preventing disease outbreaks depend on creating a thorough health and management strategy. This covers routine veterinarian care, immunization schedules, parasite prevention, and emergency readiness.

Making decisions and managing the farm can also benefit from the implementation of record-keeping systems to monitor herd performance, financial transactions, and production statistics.

Long-term productivity and sustainability of a Zebu farm can be achieved by farmers through proactive management methods, strategic planning, and effective resource usage.

CHAPTER TWO

STARTING A ZEBU FARMING BUSINESS

CHOOSING THE CORRECT ZEBU BREED

The appropriate breed selection is essential for success in Zebu farming. Characteristics like size, temperament, milk output, and illness resistance differ throughout Zebu breeds. One well-liked breed is the Brahman, which is renowned for producing meat of excellent quality, being pest-resistant, and adapting to many climates. Additionally, Brahman cattle are renowned for having a mild temperament, which makes them simpler to handle, particularly for newbies.

The Gir is a well-known Zebu breed that is highly valued for both its excellent milk yield and capacity to survive in hot, humid areas. Gir cattle are suited for dairy farming because of their reputation for being submissive. The Sahiwal is a great option for anyone who is looking for dual-purpose breeds. Sahiwal cattle are a flexible choice for farmers because of their reputation for producing a lot of milk and their resilience in challenging conditions.

It is crucial to investigate and comprehend the unique needs and traits of every Zebu breed before making a choice. The environment, the intended use (meat, milk, or dual use), the resources that are accessible, and the demand in the market should all be taken into account when choosing the best Zebu breed for your farm.

PUTTING UP APPROPRIATE FACILITIES AND HOUSING

For Zebu cattle to be healthy and productive, appropriate housing and facilities must be built. The housing should offer defense against inclement weather, including intense heat, freezing temperatures, wind, and rain.

To avoid respiratory problems and keep the cattle in a comfortable environment, proper ventilation is essential. The animals should also have ample room to move around freely in their home.

Another crucial component of establishing infrastructure for Zebu farming is adequate fencing. To keep cattle from straying or entering undesirable regions, fences assist in configuring them within predetermined zones.

The size of the herd, the terrain, and the budget will all affect the sort of fence that is employed. Electric fencing works well to keep animals inside borders and discourage predators.

Facilities including feeding areas, watering stations, and handling equipment should be positioned strategically for ease of use and efficiency in addition to housing and fencing. Your Zebu farming endeavor will be more successful overall if these facilities are well-planned and built.

KNOWING ZEBU FEEDING AND NUTRITION

For Zebu cattle to be healthy and productive, they must have a proper diet. It's crucial to comprehend their dietary needs and put in place a balanced food schedule.

Roughage, such as hay, grass, and silage, provides fiber for zebu cattle. Concentrates, like grains and supplements, provide energy and protein.

To ascertain the nutrient content of the feed and make the required modifications to fulfill the nutritional requirements of the cattle, it is crucial to regularly analyze the soil and forage. It's also essential to always have access to fresh, clean water for good digestion and general wellness.

Meals should be fed according to regular timetables, with equal distribution throughout the day. Keeping an eye on the cattle's body condition score helps guarantee they are getting enough food without becoming overweight or underweight.

When creating an ideal meal plan for Zebu cattle, it can be helpful to seek advice from a nutritionist or veterinarian on the cattle's age, gender, reproductive status, and amount of activity.

ZEBU'S HEALTH AND CARE MANAGEMENT

For farming to be successful, maintaining the health and welfare of Zebu cattle must come first. Deworming, immunizations, and routine health examinations are crucial procedures for preventing infections and parasites. It is very advised to create a thorough health management plan in close collaboration with a veterinarian.

Disease prevention depends heavily on maintaining good hygiene and sanitation in living spaces, feeding places, and water supplies. The danger of bacterial and fungal infections can be decreased by promptly removing manure and washing and disinfecting equipment regularly.

It is important to take mental and emotional well-being into account in addition to physical health. Enrichment activities that lower stress and improve general welfare include providing scratching posts, shelter, and opportunities for socialization with other cattle. When calves exhibit symptoms of distress or disease, it is possible to identify these behaviors and act quickly to provide necessary care.

ZEBU BREEDING METHODS

Using efficient breeding methods is crucial to keeping the Zebu herd robust and productive. Successful breeding of Zebu cattle depends on an understanding of their reproductive cycle, which includes estrus detection, mating, and pregnancy diagnosis. Maintaining precise records of pedigrees, breeding dates, and medical history facilitates tracking the herd's development and ancestry.

A popular breeding method that enables the selective breeding of desired qualities including milk output, meat quality, and disease resistance is artificial insemination, or AI.

Successful artificial insemination (AI) depends on handling and storing semen properly as well as synchronizing insemination with the cow's estrus cycle.

Another method of breeding is natural mating, in which a bull is brought into the herd to mate with cows who are willing. The development of better offspring with desired genetic features is ensured by a careful selection process. Pregnancy testing methods, including rectal palpation or ultrasound, are used to monitor fetal development and confirm pregnancies.

Adopting good breeding procedures enhances the overall viability and sustainability of Zebu farming operations, as do appropriate diet, health care, and environmental factors. Optimizing productivity and profitability in Zebu cattle farming is made possible by the regular assessment and enhancement of breeding techniques based on market demand and performance.

28

CHAPTER THREE

ZEBU FARMING METHODS

ACTIVITIES AND DAILY SCHEDULES ON A ZEBU FARM

Setting up a planned timetable for daily chores and routines on a Zebu farm is essential for productivity and the welfare of the animals. The Zebus are usually fed and watered first thing in the morning to make sure they have access to a nutritious, well-balanced diet and clean, fresh water.

Regular health checks should be incorporated into the schedule, along with immunizations, injury treatment as soon as possible, and watching out for any symptoms of the disease. It's also essential to keep the Zebus's living quarters tidy and comfortable, which calls for routinely cleaning the pens or barns and giving enough bedding for the animals' comfort and hygienic needs.

Grooming, clipping hooves, and addressing any issues about reproduction or breeding may come up during the day. Zebus must be handled carefully and gently, using the right tools and methods to reduce anxiety for the animals and the handlers. Regular training sessions can also improve overall farm operations and safety procedures by making Zebus more controllable and command-responsive. Finally, keeping daily records of observations, treatments, and activities is essential for monitoring the Zebu herd's health, spotting trends, and making well-informed decisions.

SEASONAL UPKEEP AND CARE

Successful Zebu farming necessitates seasonal care and maintenance, which calls for flexibility and awareness to deal with changing environmental circumstances all year round. As pastures become ready for grazing in the spring, attention turns to testing the soil, applying fertilizer as needed, and making sure there is enough pasture rotation to avoid overgrazing. Breeding chances also arise throughout this season; to maximize breeding outcomes and herd genetics, meticulous planning and monitoring of reproductive cycles is necessary.

The problems of summer include managing Zebus's heat discomfort by giving him plenty of shade, water sources to drink, and feeding schedules that coincide with cooler times of the day.

During this period, it is especially important to implement pest management strategies, such as fly control and routine health examinations to minimize any possible problems. Fall brings with it the need to prepare for winter by storing feed, strengthening shelter structures, and keeping an eye out for any indications of cold stress or malnourishment in Zebus.

Zebu nutrition needs to be especially focused on the winter months when they need to consume enough calories and nutrients to stay healthy and resist the lower temperatures.

Zebus must be protected from severe cold conditions with enough bedding and shelter, as well as by taking precautions against water freezing and making sure that unfrozen water sources are accessible. Regular check-ups are still important, and respiratory conditions and other cold-related illnesses require extra attention. Farmers may maximize herd health and productivity all year round by using seasonal care techniques designed specifically for Zebu farming.

TAKING CARE OF ZEBU PASTURES AND GRAZING

Maintaining soil health, increasing fodder consumption, and preserving a healthy ecology on the farm all depend on the management of zebu grazing and pastures. A key technique in preventing overgrazing and promoting forage regrowth is rotational grazing, which entails splitting pastures into smaller paddocks and rotating Zebus regularly. This tactic enhances the ecosystem's nutrient cycle, minimizes soil erosion, and encourages better grasses.

Maintaining pasture health requires regular soil testing to determine pH balance and nutrient levels, applying fertilization plans based on soil analysis, and quickly resolving any issues with invasive species or weeds. To prevent pasture degradation and encourage sustainable forage development, grazing management plans should be adjusted to account for seasonal variations in stocking rates and grazing duration.

By including a range of forage plants, pasture resilience and nutrition for Zebus can be improved, providing grazing opportunities all year round. To guarantee that Zebus has access to clean drinking water in every paddock and to minimize soil erosion near water sources, water management is also essential.

Zebu farmers may maximize the quality of their feed, maintain thriving ecosystems, and advance long-term sustainability on their farms by putting into practice efficient grazing and pasture management techniques.

ECOLOGICAL METHODS IN ZEBU AGRICULTURE

Modern Zebu farming must embrace sustainable methods to reduce its negative effects on the environment and ensure its long-term viability. Reducing waste and guaranteeing water supply during dry periods can be achieved by putting into practice water conservation measures including rainwater collecting, effective irrigation systems, and appropriate water management in animal watering places. Further lowering carbon emissions and energy expenses is achieved by using renewable energy sources, such as wind turbines and solar panels, for farm activities.

Additionally, using integrated pest management (IPM) strategies encourages the use of natural pest control measures while reducing the need for chemical pesticides. This entails cultivating trap crops, introducing helpful insects, and preserving robust soil ecosystems. Agroforestry techniques, such as planting trees in pasture regions, enhance soil health, biodiversity, and carbon sequestration in addition to giving Zebus shade and windbreaks. Finally, maintaining wildlife habitat, rotating crops, and encouraging biodiversity all contribute to ecological balance and resilience on farms.

MAINTAINING DOCUMENTS AND MANAGING DATA

Efficient documentation and data administration are key components of prosperous Zebu farming endeavors.

Keep thorough records of every Zebu's medical history, including shots, dewormings, veterinary appointments, and any ailments or wounds. When necessary, this information enables prompt interventions and aids in the monitoring of each animal's health. To guarantee balanced meals and maximize production, keep detailed records of feeding schedules, including feed kinds, volumes, and nutritional content.

Financial aspects are included in record-keeping as well. Maintain a record of all feed, medication, equipment, and labor costs to evaluate profitability and pinpoint areas where savings can be made.

A herd's reproductive success, weight increase, and milk yield are examples of production metrics that can be monitored. This information can be used to make decisions about herd management, breeding, and culling tactics.

Data collection, analysis, and reporting procedures can be streamlined by utilizing digital tools and software intended for farm management.

This includes efficiently organizing and interpreting data using databases, spreadsheets, or specialist farm management software. Maintaining accuracy and relevancy of data is essential to making sure your Zebu farm runs smoothly and continues to comply with regulations. Review and update records regularly.

CHAPTER FOUR

ZEBU VETERINARY AND HEALTH SERVICES

COMMON HEALTH PROBLEMS AND SYMPTOMS IN ZEBU

Like any other livestock, zebu cattle are susceptible to several health problems that may affect their general well-being and output. Comprehending these prevalent medical conditions and identifying their indications is essential for efficient handling. Tick infestation is a common health issue in Zebu, as it can cause skin irritation, anemia, and decreased weight increase. Respiratory infections, such as pneumonia, which can cause coughing, nasal discharge, and difficulty breathing, are other frequent problems. Furthermore, incorrect feeding practices or abrupt dietary changes might result in digestive issues like bloat or acidosis, which can cause discomfort and a decrease in feed consumption.

Early intervention and treatment for various health disorders depend on the ability to recognize their signs.

Look for signs of hair loss, increased scratching, and ticks on the skin or in the ears when you suspect a tick infestation. Coughing, nasal discharge, and wheezing are symptoms of respiratory infections; bloating, decreased appetite, and changes in the consistency of feces are markers of digestive problems. You can keep your Zebu herd safe and prevent these problems from getting worse by keeping an eye on them and acting quickly.

Maintaining Zebu's health requires putting preventive measures into practice. Regular de worming and tick control measures are part of this to lower parasite burdens and lower the chance of infections. You should incorporate vaccination programs against common diseases like clostridial infections and respiratory infections into your preventative healthcare plan. A balanced diet, fresh water, and suitable housing can also strengthen their immune systems and lower their risk of developing health problems. To further improve the health and productivity of your Zebu herd, schedule regular check-ups and consultations with veterinarians for customized health plans.

IMMUNIZATION AND HEALTH PREVENTION

For Zebu cattle, vaccination is essential for preventing infectious illnesses and enhancing general health. Effective disease prevention requires knowing the immunization schedule and giving vaccinations as prescribed. Important immunizations for Zebu include those against clostridial illnesses like blackleg and respiratory illnesses including infectious bovine rhinotracheitis (IBR) and bovine viral diarrhea (BVD). By boosting protection against common infections, these vaccinations lower the likelihood of illness outbreaks in your herd.

It's critical to adhere to manufacturer guidelines for vaccine delivery, handling, and storage while starting a vaccination regimen. The effectiveness of vaccinations is ensured by keeping them stored at the proper temperature and shielding them from light.

Tracking immunity levels and scheduling booster injections efficiently are made easier by following dosage recommendations for vaccinations and keeping thorough records of every immunization received. For the best possible preventative healthcare, you should also regularly examine and update your vaccination protocol based on the health status of the herd and the prevalence of the disease.

Preventive healthcare for Zebu encompasses not only immunizations but also regular health examinations, management of nutrition, control of parasites, and environmental hygiene. Zebu health markers, such as body condition score, weight increase, and behavior, should be regularly monitored to enable early identification of health problems and prompt treatment. Disinfection procedures and quarantine guidelines for arriving animals are two examples of biosecurity measures that are put into place to assist stop the entry and spread of disease. Working together with vets to get advice on preventive care plans customized to your

Zebu herd's unique requirements improves general health and output.

CONTROL OF PARASITES IN ZEBU

For Zebu's health and productivity to be maintained, effective parasite management is necessary. Reduced feed efficiency, weight loss, anemia, and heightened susceptibility to various illnesses are all consequences of parasitic infestations. Comprehending the life cycles of parasites, determining risk factors, and putting preventive measures in place are all necessary for developing a thorough parasite management program. Internal parasites like gastrointestinal worms and exterior parasites like ticks and mites are common parasites that affect Zebu.

Regular de worming with anthelmintic medications—which are effective against internal parasites—is a crucial part of parasite control. To create a de worming regimen that takes into account the size of the herd, the conditions of the pasture, and the patterns of parasite resistance, consult with veterinarians.

Monitoring parasite numbers and adjusting de worming techniques as necessary can be facilitated by rotating dewormers and performing fecal egg counts. Furthermore, incorporating pasture management techniques including manure management, rotational grazing, and pasture rest intervals can lower parasite loads and restrict their spread.

Using management methods like acaricide treatments and pasture sprays can assist lower infestations of external parasites like ticks and mites. Zebu can benefit from early detection and focused treatment when routinely checked for symptoms of external parasites, such as skin sores, hair loss, and discomfort. Reducing overcrowding and giving Zebu access to dry, clean resting places can also help with parasite control? The best way to manage parasites in your Zebu herd is to work together with veterinarians and parasitologists for advice on parasite detection, control methods, and monitoring procedures.

HANDLING EMERGENCIES AND INJURIES

In Zebu farming, injuries and emergencies can happen without warning. Prompt and efficient management is necessary to protect animal welfare and avoid complications. Cuts, bruises, fractures, and lameness from fights, accidents, or environmental risks are among the common injuries in Zebu. Having a fully stocked first aid kit, familiarity with fundamental veterinary care, and the ability to seek veterinarian assistance when necessary are all necessary components of emergency preparedness.

When an animal is injured, the first steps in treating it include determining how serious the damage is, cleaning and bandaging the wound, and, if required, separating the wounded animal from the others. Minimal injuries should be treated as a way to encourage quicker healing and avoid infection. It is imperative to consult a veterinarian for a competent assessment and treatment in cases of more severe injuries or emergencies, such as difficult calvings or unexpected infections. During emergencies, keeping composed and communicating well reduces stress for both the animal and the handler and promotes effective medical care.

In Zebu, preventive actions can also lower the chance of accidents and medical issues. Potential risks can be reduced by making sure there are secure handling facilities, appropriate fencing, enough room for mobility, and routine equipment maintenance. Enhancing preparedness and reaction capacities is achieved by training farm personnel in animal handling practices, emergency response protocols, and fundamental veterinary care protocols. To further improve your farm's preparedness to handle injuries and crises, work with nearby veterinary facilities and create an emergency action plan that is specific to your needs.

CHAPTER FIVE
BREEDING AND REPRODUCTION OF ZEBU
RECOGNIZING THE REPRODUCTIVE CYCLES OF ZEBU

Understanding the unique reproductive cycles of zebu is crucial to their successful farming. The estrous cycle, which has four phases—proestrus, estrus, metestrus, and diestrus—is the main focus of these cycles. The commencement of the cow's reproductive organs getting ready for ovulation is known as proestrus. This stage is critical for tracking behavioral changes that signal the cow is approaching estrus, the time when she is more receptive to mating, such as increased restlessness or mounting activity.

Breeding during estrus, which happens roughly every 21 days, is essential for effective fertilization. Farmers can determine the best time for insemination by being aware of the symptoms of estrus, which include mounting behavior and clear vaginal discharge. The next phase is called metastasis, during which the corpus luteum, a transitory endocrine structure that is essential for preserving pregnancy in the event of fertilization, forms. Diestrus, in conclusion, denotes the non-receptive stage before the subsequent proestrus.

BREEDING PROCEDURES AND STRATEGIES

In zebu farming, a variety of breeding strategies and tactics are used, each with pros and downsides. To replicate natural processes, bulls and cows must be allowed to mate freely during natural mating. While this is a simple process, it does involve careful selection of bulls for desired qualities and compatibility with other animals. Contrarily, artificial insemination (AI) provides exact control over genetics and disease prevention, which is essential for raising the productivity and quality of herds.

Another cutting-edge method that makes it possible to widely reproduce superior genetics is embryo transfer (ET). To facilitate gestation, embryos from genetically superior cows are harvested and inserted into surrogate cows.

This strategy speeds genetic advancement but requires specific equipment and skill. Additionally, because of their accuracy and effectiveness in breeding programs, cutting-edge reproductive technologies like sexed semen and in vitro fertilization (IVF) are becoming more and more popular.

PREGNANCY MANAGEMENT AND CARE

For zebu cows and their progeny to be healthy and happy, proper pregnancy care and management are essential. It's critical to track the cow's pregnancy development following a successful insemination. Pregnancy care includes regular veterinary examinations, nutritional modifications, and parasite control. Pregnant cows should have pleasant accommodations and enough space to reduce stress and encourage ideal fetal growth.

As the pregnancy goes on, the focus turns to getting ready for calving. It is imperative to establish a calving management strategy, provide sufficient nourishment, and maintain a clean and safe calving environment.

Ensuring a smooth delivery procedure involves keeping a keen eye out for indications that labor is imminent in the cow. Post-calving care entails keeping an eye out for any health concerns with the cow and the calf, administering any required vaccines, and starting the newborn's early bonding and feeding.

ZEBU CALVES' BIRTH AND NEONATAL CARE

To guarantee their health and survival, zebu calves need close attention both during and after delivery. When difficulties arise during delivery or other issues arise, the calving process should be continuously watched and assistance should be provided if needed. Keeping the newborn calf clean and warm helps shield it from diseases and hypothermia. The calf's immune system is strengthened through passive immunity transmission, which depends on immediate colostrum ingestion.

Regular check-ups, immunization schedules, and dietary control are all part of neonatal care. In addition to lowering death rates, keeping an eye out for symptoms of illness or weakness and acting quickly to address them increases calf growth. For calf development, adequate housing, access to clean water, and feed are necessary. Calf health and overall herd productivity are further improved by putting disease prevention strategies and appropriate cleanliness practices into effect.

STRATEGIES FOR GENETIC IMPROVEMENT

Strategies for genetic improvement are essential for raising the productivity and quality of zebu herds. The goal of selective breeding is to increase desirable qualities like temperament, illness resistance, and milk output by marrying genetically superior bulls and cows. Genetic testing and pedigree analysis are two technologies that help find the best candidates for breeding operations.

Zebu cattle are crossed with other breeds to create hybrid vigor and novel genetic features. The management of crossbred offspring and the careful selection of appropriate breeds are key factors in improving herd health.

A novel method called genomic selection makes use of DNA data to precisely estimate an animal's genetic worth. By recognizing exceptional animals at an early stage of development, this method expedites genetic advancement.

To put these genetic improvement ideas into practice, rigorous record-keeping, data analysis, and cooperation with breed groups and veterinary professionals are needed. Over time, sustained herd improvement is ensured through ongoing assessment and modification of breeding objectives and procedures.

CHAPTER SIX

ZEBU MANAGEMENT AND PRODUCTION

PRODUCTION OF MILK AND MANAGEMENT OF DAIRIES

Dairy management in zebu farming involves a range of important activities to maintain optimal milk output and quality. The health and welfare of the zebu livestock must come first. Providing a balanced meal full of essential elements like protein, vitamins, and minerals is one way to do this. A veterinarian's routine examinations are also necessary to keep an eye on the herd's general health and to quickly handle any problems.

Next, the secret to optimizing milk output is to use efficient milking techniques. This involves keeping the cows' udders and milking apparatus clean to avoid contamination. Carefully and quickly milking the animals is the best way to guarantee full milk extraction without making them uncomfortable. To preserve milk's freshness and quality, storing must be done correctly.

Record-keeping is essential for managing dairy farms. Making educated decisions for the herd is facilitated by keeping thorough records of milk production, medical interventions, breeding cycles, and other pertinent data. Overall milk quality and the profitability of the dairy business are also impacted by the adoption of excellent hygiene measures throughout the dairy farm, such as clean water supplies and sanitary living facilities for the cattle.

MEAT PROCESSING AND QUALITY CONTROL

To guarantee high-quality meat and the general health of the herd, zebu farming for meat production entails several procedures. First and foremost, it's critical to choose robust, genetically superior zebra breeds that are renowned for their high-quality meat and rapid growth. A balanced diet provides necessary nutrients for muscle development and general health, which is important for meat production.

It's crucial to regularly check on the health and well-being of the herd to identify and quickly treat any health problems. This covers shots, managing parasites, and routine veterinary examinations. Meat quality and general farm hygiene are enhanced by utilizing hygienic housing and handling procedures for cattle.

Humane handling and killing procedures are crucial in the meat industry. The animals will experience the least amount of stress when slaughtered humanely and ethically, maintaining the quality of the meat. Appropriate methods for preparing and storing meat further ensure that the meat is safe and fresh for consumers.

HARVESTING WOOL AND FIBER FROM ZEBU

To produce high-quality fibers, zebu farming for wool and fiber harvesting necessitates meticulous management and grooming techniques. The cleanliness and caliber of the zebu cattle's wool or fiber are preserved through regular grooming. This involves trimming and brushing wool at the proper intervals to get rid of extra and avoid matting.

The quality of the wool and fiber that zebu animals generate is also influenced by proper nutrition. Strong fibers and healthy hair growth are encouraged by a diet high in protein and vital minerals. Furthermore, giving the cattle a tidy and comfortable living space lowers stress levels and enhances the caliber of their wool or fiber.

Careful shearing methods are needed to harvest wool or fiber from zebu calves to produce long, consistent strands.

After being gathered, the wool or fiber is processed to make finished goods like yarn or textiles. This process includes washing, spinning, and weaving. Wool and fiber must be stored properly to preserve their quality and guard against moisture and bug damage.

VALUE-ENHANCED ZEBU GOODS

Beyond meat and dairy, zebu farming offers potential for value-added products. Zebu leather, which is renowned for its strength and quality, is one such item.

Effective handling of zebu hides, encompassing tanning and processing methods, can yield high-quality leather goods for several sectors.

Organic fertilizer is another product with added value that comes from zebu growing. Sustainable agricultural practices are encouraged and soil fertility is improved by applying zebu manure as a natural fertilizer. Organic fertilizers made from zebu are safe and effective as long as they are composted and applied properly.

Zebu farming can also result in the production of biofuels from the waste of cattle, which adds to the availability of renewable energy sources.

Cutting-edge methods for turning zebu garbage into biogas or other biofuels provide environmentally friendly energy production options that are both sustainable and low-impact.

ZEBU FARMING'S MARKETING AND SALES STRATEGIES

Zebu farming requires strong marketing and sales techniques to be successful. To customize items to fulfill market demand, target markets, and consumer preferences must be identified. Zebu products can have a greater reach and visibility through the use of digital marketing tools and platforms.

Maintaining a solid rapport with distributors and customers is essential for steady sales growth. Gaining the trust and loyalty of customers is achieved through competitive pricing, quality control, and superior customer service. Networking with possible partners and showcasing Zebu products are two further benefits of attending trade fairs and industry gatherings.

Expanding market reach and accessibility can also be achieved by diversifying sales methods, such as direct-to-consumer platforms and online marketplaces.

CHAPTER SEVEN

ENVIRONMENTAL FACTORS IN ZEBU AGRICULTURE

ECOLOGICAL FARMING METHODS

Implementing techniques like rotational grazing can maximize land utilization and stop soil erosion in sustainable zebu farming. Rotating pastures improves soil fertility and lowers erosion by allowing grass to regrow. Legumes are excellent cover crops because they fix nitrogen, which lessens the need for artificial fertilizers and increases biodiversity.

Putting water-saving measures into practice is essential. This includes the use of drought-resistant crops, and effective irrigation techniques including drip irrigation, and rainwater collection.

Efficient handling of waste, such as turning manure into organic fertilizer by composting it, reduces environmental effects while optimizing resource use.

By encouraging the use of natural pest control strategies like introducing beneficial insects or setting traps, integrated pest management (IPM) techniques lessen the need for pesticides. This sustainable strategy maintains the farm's ecological balance and safeguards the health of the zebus, promoting resilience and long-term survival.

POLLUTION CONTROL AND WASTE MANAGEMENT

The production of nutrient-rich organic fertilizer through composting manure is one strategy used in zebu farming to effectively manage waste. This lessens the need for chemical fertilizers, absorbs odors, and enhances the health of the soil. Pollution to the environment is reduced by properly disposing of non-biodegradable waste, such as plastics and packing materials.

Managing runoff from agricultural operations is one way to implement pollution control measures and avoid contaminating water supplies. Water quality can be preserved by installing sediment traps, vegetation buffers, and erosion control structures, which can greatly minimize soil erosion and nutrient flow into water bodies.

Farm operations that use renewable energy sources, such as wind turbines or solar panels, become less dependent on fossil fuels, which lowers greenhouse gas emissions. This sustainable energy strategy promotes a better and cleaner farming ecosystem in line with environmental conservation objectives.

PRESERVATION OF NATURAL RESOURCES

In zebu farming, techniques like agroforestry—where trees are deliberately grown to enhance soil fertility, store carbon dioxide, and offer shade for livestock—are used to conserve natural resources. This promotes climate resilience, increases biodiversity, and establishes habitats for species.

Water resources are conserved by effective water management techniques including rainwater gathering and drip irrigation, guaranteeing sustainable use for livestock and crops. By minimizing soil erosion, soil conservation practices like terracing and contour plowing help protect priceless agricultural land.

Farm operations that use renewable energy sources, such as solar electricity, become less dependent on non-renewable resources, which promotes environmental sustainability and energy conservation. Zebu farming can continue to be profitable in the long run while preserving natural habitats by implementing these resource conservation techniques.

CLIMATE MODIFICATION FOR ZEBU AGRICULTURE

The process of adapting zebu farming operations to climate change entails the selection of breeds that are tolerant to heat stress and disease difficulties. In cattle housing, installing shade structures, enough ventilation, and water misting systems help reduce heat stress during extreme weather events.

During times of water constraint, food security can be guaranteed by diversifying crops and forages to include drought-tolerant versions. Crop productivity and water utilization are maximized by putting into practice effective water management techniques like using soil moisture sensors and scheduling watering according to plant requirements.

Making better decisions and managing resources is facilitated by the use of climate-smart technologies including precision agriculture instruments, drones for crop monitoring, and weather forecasting apps. By improving farm resistance to climatic fluctuation, these adjustments guarantee viable zebu farming methods in the face of shifting environmental circumstances.

SOCIAL RESPONSIBILITY AND COMMUNITY INVOLVEMENT

To engage local populations in zebu farming, it is necessary to respect indigenous knowledge, work toward sustainable land use practices, and advance socioeconomic development. Communities are empowered and local livelihoods are improved via the use of fair labor practices and training opportunities.

Encouraging community involvement and ownership in agricultural ventures is achieved through funding education and awareness campaigns about environmental conservation, animal welfare, and sustainable farming practices. The neighboring towns and farm laborers both gain from infrastructure investments made in things like water supply systems and medical facilities.

Positive relationships and goodwill are fostered via participation in social responsibility programs, such as providing support to nearby schools, healthcare facilities, and community development projects. This focus on the community not only helps the zebu farming business but also enhances the general wealth and well-being of the surrounding area.

CHAPTER EIGHT
REGULATORY AND LEGAL ASPECTS
RECOGNIZING THE REGULATIONS FOR ZEBU FARMING

Like any other agricultural endeavor, zebu farming is governed by several laws that cover different facets of the business. For newcomers to ensure compliance and seamless operations, they must comprehend these requirements. Zoning laws, which specify the locations and methods of agricultural activity, are an important factor. This covers zoning regulation compliance, environmental impact evaluations, and land use concerns. To ensure sustainable and environmentally friendly operations, there are also laws regarding the use of water, waste management, and the application of pesticides and herbicides.

Regulations about zebu farming's animal welfare are another crucial topic. These rules include things like the need for veterinary care, housing needs, transit guidelines, and humane handling techniques.

To protect their zebu herd's welfare and to stay out of trouble with the law, novices should get familiar with these rules. Furthermore, keeping breeding records and genetic variety within the herd depends on a grasp of the laws governing breeding procedures, including those about genetic testing and documentation needs.

ZEBU FARMS' LICENSES & PERMITS

To maintain legal compliance and efficient operations, running a zebu farm necessitates obtaining several licenses and permissions. Beginners must comprehend the various licenses and permits that are needed, including those for environmental protection, animal breeding, and agricultural operations. To prevent delays or fines, it is essential to fully comprehend the requirements and apply on time for these permissions, which frequently involve applications, inspections, and fees.

In addition, zoning permissions can be required based on the zebu farm's location and local laws. These licenses often specify the acceptable uses of the land for farming, including zebu cultivation, and they could also impose rules and regulations. To maintain compliance with food safety and quality requirements, beginners should also be aware of any particular permissions or certificates needed for selling zebu products, such as meat or dairy.

OBSERVANCE OF LAWS CONCERNING ANIMAL WELFARE

Zebu farming requires strict adherence to standards regarding animal care. These regulations include many facets of animal care, housing, and management to guarantee the humane treatment of animals. Novices should become acquainted with these legal frameworks, which may cover aspects such as sufficient food, uncontaminated water availability, suitable housing, and veterinary treatment.

Moreover, regulations about animal welfare frequently specify requirements for handling and transportation methods to reduce stress and guarantee the welfare of zebu cattle.

Respecting these laws preserves the sustainability and good name of the Zebu farming enterprise in addition to reflecting ethical farming methods. Beginners in Zebu farming must maintain thorough records and follow best practices because regular inspections and audits may be performed to evaluate compliance.

FINANCIAL REPORTING AND TAXATION

Like any other business, zebu farming must comply with financial reporting and tax regulations. Tax rules about agricultural activities, such as income tax, property tax, and sales tax on zebu products, should be familiar to beginners. To guarantee compliance and optimize tax advantages, like depreciation of assets and farm expense deductions, it is recommended to maintain precise financial documentation and collaborate with a proficient accountant.

Furthermore, assessing the sustainability and profitability of the zebu farming enterprise depends on having a solid understanding of financial reporting regulations.

This entails keeping track of all income, outlays, stock, and asset depreciation. A beginner should also be aware of any tax breaks or subsidies that are offered for farming activities. These can differ based on the state and the policies of the government. In addition to meeting legal requirements, appropriate financial reporting and administration promote wise decision-making and the long-term viability of zebu cultivation.

ZEBU FARMS' INSURANCE

For zebu farms, insurance is essential to risk management since it offers protection against unanticipated events that can interrupt operations or result in losses. Initiators ought to investigate various forms of insurance coverage specifically designed for zebu farming, including crop insurance for pasture or forage crops, liability insurance for farm accidents or injuries, and property insurance for structures, machinery, and livestock.

Specialized insurance solutions, including covering for genetic loss or animal mortality insurance, might also be offered for certain risks associated with zebu farming. It is crucial to comprehend the policy terms, premiums, claims procedures, and coverage scope while choosing the appropriate insurance solutions to successfully reduce risks. To guarantee complete safety and peace of mind for newcomers to the business, it is recommended that insurance policies be reviewed regularly and that coverage be updated when the zebu farming operation expands or changes.

CHAPTER NINE

TYPICAL WORRIES IN ZEBU FARMING

HANDLING PREDATORS OF ZEBU TYPE

Controlling predators is essential to the security and welfare of the animals in zebu farming. Installing strong fencing around the farm's perimeter and employing wire mesh or electric fencing to keep predators out is one efficient way to do this. Using guard animals, like dogs or llamas, can also assist deter predators because these animals are innately oriented to defend their herd and its individuals from harm. Reducing the number of traits that appeal to predators—for example, by not leaving out potential food sources—is another tactic.

Furthermore, nocturnal predators can be deterred from entering the farm by strategically placing illumination. In this sense, solar-powered lighting or motion-activated lights can work well. To stop predator intrusions, it's also critical to routinely check the perimeter for any fencing breaches or weak places and to fix them right once. More assistance in handling more enduring predator problems can be obtained by working with regional wildlife agencies or by employing expert pest control services.

MANAGING ZEBU'S AGGRESSIVE BEHAVIOR

Farmers may encounter difficulties as a result of aggressive behavior in Zebus, but dangers can be reduced by being aware of and using proper handling procedures. First and foremost, it's critical to identify aggressive cues, like heightened hackles, stomping, or vocalizations, and to react coolly and firmly in response. Since Zebus are herd animals that respond well to established leadership, creating a hierarchy among the herd through consistent handling and training can also help lessen violent behavior.

Furthermore, giving animals enough room and resources—like distinct feeding areas—can reduce rivalry and hostility. Aggression can be discouraged and desired actions can be encouraged by using strategies like positive reinforcement training.

A veterinarian or animal behaviorist may need to be consulted in cases of persistent aggressiveness to evaluate any underlying causes, such as pain or hormonal imbalances that may be influencing aggressive behaviors.

CONTROLLING DISEASE OUTBREAKS

In Zebu farming, effective disease control is essential to preserving the health and production of the herd. Disease transmission can be halted by putting in place biosecurity measures like limiting access to the farm to authorized individuals, putting new animals in quarantine before reintroducing them to the herd, and routinely cleaning premises and equipment. Furthermore, hygienic practices, such as donning protective gear and washing hands after handling various animals, lessen the possibility of virus transmission.

Disease prevention requires routine health monitoring, including adhering to veterinarian-recommended vaccination and de worming schedules.

Containment efforts during outbreaks can be accelerated by creating a thorough disease response strategy that outlines procedures for identifying, isolating, and treating sick animals. Keeping up with diseases that are common in the area and working with veterinary professionals can help improve disease control plans even further.

WEATHER AND DROUGHT ISSUES

Zebu farming involves a lot of managing drought and unfavorable weather, especially in areas where these issues are common. Water conservation measures, including constructing effective irrigation systems or collecting rainwater, can guarantee that the herd will always have access to water during dry seasons.

It is also possible to lessen the negative effects of drought on animal nutrition by using drought-resistant forage and feed options.

For Zebus's well-being, it is also crucial to provide them with enough shade and cover from intense heat or cold.

Minimizing animal stress can be achieved by keeping an eye on weather forecasts and modifying management strategies accordingly. Examples of these adjustments include changing grazing patterns or providing more supplemental feeding during severe weather. Creating backup preparations, including having access to emergency water sources or substitute food sources, increases resistance to weather-related difficulties.

SUSTAINING SAFETY AND SECURITY ON FARMS

It is critical to guarantee farm security and safety for the benefit of Zebus as well as the workers engaged in farming activities. Installing surveillance equipment, such as cameras or alarms, may keep an eye on the goings-on around the farm and discourage intruders. By putting in place access control mechanisms, such as visitor identity checks and guarded entrance points, security is improved, and unwanted access is avoided.

Furthermore, a safe working environment is promoted by giving farm workers the necessary tools, first aid kits, and emergency response plans, as well as proper training. Accidents and injuries are reduced by performing routine safety audits and resolving possible risks, such as uneven terrain or mechanical hazards. To further help ensure farm security and quickly resolve any security concerns, collaborating with local law enforcement or security organizations might be beneficial.

CHAPTER TEN

FAQS ABOUT ZEBU FARMING

HOW LONG DOES A ZEBU LIVE?

Similar to other breeds of cattle, zebuses vary in length of life based on hereditary, environmental, and managerial factors. A Zebu can live anywhere from 18 to 25 years on average if given the right care and diet. Some, on the other hand, may live longer—in extreme circumstances, up to 30 years or longer.

Your Zebus needs balanced food, routine veterinary treatment, and a cozy living space if you want to guarantee a long and healthy life for them. This involves having enough room for grazing and exercise, as well as having access to clean water and suitable protection from inclement weather. Furthermore, controlling stressors like animal aggression or overpopulation might improve the animals' general health and lifespan.

Planning your farm management tactics, including breeding programs, medical procedures, and retirement plans for older animals, requires an understanding of the Zebus lifespan. You can increase their output and help create a profitable and long-lasting Zebu farming enterprise by putting their well-being first and attending to their unique demands as they age.

WHAT IS THE REQUIRED AREA FOR A ZEBU FARM?

A Zebu farm's space needs are determined by several variables, including the quantity of animals, the way they graze, and the resources that are accessible. Generally speaking, depending on the condition of the pasture and the methods used for supplemental feeding, it is advised to set aside between 2 and 5 acres of land for each Zebu.

To meet Zebus's nutritional needs and maximize space use, pasture management must be done correctly. By alternating the animals between many paddocks, rotational grazing promotes grass regeneration and inhibits overgrazing, guaranteeing a steady and sustainable supply of food.

Moreover, shelter and specific spaces for grazing, drinking, and sleeping can increase productivity and reduce environmental effects.

Think about things like geography, soil quality, water availability, and fencing needs while designing the layout of your Zebu farm. Not only does sufficient room allow Zebus to grow and develop healthily, but it also makes it easier to manage the herd effectively through handling, breeding, and other activities. You can establish a profitable and environmentally responsible Zebu farming enterprise by making the most use of available area and putting good land management techniques into effect.

WHAT DISTINGUISHES ZEBU CATTLE FROM OTHER KINDS OF CATTLE?

In comparison to other cattle breeds, zebu cattle, which are distinguished by their drooping ears, humped back, and heat endurance, display several notable distinctions. Their capacity to withstand hot and muggy weather is one of their most remarkable traits, which makes them ideal for tropical areas where other breeds would suffer. Their distinct hump, which stores fat and aids in controlling body temperature, is thought to be the cause of their heat tolerance.

Zebus temperaments are often associated with being submissive and flexible to different management styles. Due to their resistance to illnesses and parasites, they are frequently chosen over other breeds because they require less frequent and extensive veterinary treatment. Zebus are also useful for breeding operations because of their high reproductive rates and maternal instincts.

Zebus may differ from other breeds in terms of productivity in terms of growth rates, meat quality, and milk production. These variations may affect the breed selection for particular farming goals, such as dairy production, meat production, or crossbreeding initiatives. To manage livestock and raise cattle, it is crucial to comprehend the special qualities and skills of Zebus in contrast to other breeds.

CAN ZEBU LIVE IN A VARIETY OF CLIMATES?

Zebus are well known for their capacity to flourish in a variety of climates, from semi-arid to tropical. They can tolerate high temperatures and humidity levels because of their innate climatic adaptability to hot, humid conditions and heat-tolerance strategies like perspiring and sweating. Zebu farming is therefore appropriate in areas with long summers and little winter.

Zebus has clear advantages over non-adapted breeds in tropical settings where heat stress can affect animal health and productivity. Their resilience and sustainability in such situations are largely attributed to their capacity to make effective use of the forage and water resources that are available, as well as their resistance to some diseases that are common in warmer climates.

The provision of shade, water accessibility, and nutritional supplements are examples of good management techniques that further enhance Zebus' capacity to flourish in a variety of climates.

Zebus thrive in hot, muggy weather, but with the right care and attention, they may even adapt to more moderate climes. They are flexible for farmers working in areas with different seasonal variations and climate patterns because of their adaptability. Farmers can enhance their farming techniques and optimize Zebus's potential for success in various environmental settings by comprehending the breed's unique climatic requirements and obstacles.

WHEN COMPARING ZEBU FARMING TO OTHER LIVESTOCK, HOW PROFITABLE IS IT?

When compared to other livestock, the profitability of Zebu farming is contingent upon several elements, such as market demand, production costs, management strategies, and local economic situations. Zebus are prized for their meat, milk, and hide; variables including quantity, quality, and customer preferences affect market prices.

Farmers that produce meat can profit greatly from favorable market pricing in areas where Zebu meat is in strong demand, whether for domestic consumption or export markets. Similar to this, Zebu milk, which is prized for both its high-fat content and nutritional value, maybe a lucrative venture, particularly when turned into goods with additional value like yogurt or cheese?

However, effective production techniques including herd management, breeding plans, nutrition optimization, disease control, and marketing plans are all essential to the financial success of zebu farming. A prosperous Zebu farming enterprise necessitates minimizing production costs, optimizing yields, and exploiting dependable markets.

When comparing Zebu farming to other livestock endeavors like sheep, dairy, or beef farming, a thorough examination of market trends, risk considerations, and input-output dynamics is necessary. Zebus has clear advantages in terms of resilience, adaptability, and product diversity, but depending on specific farm conditions and company plans, the profitability equation may change.

When compared to alternative livestock options, Zebu farming operations can have higher profitability and sustainability through the implementation of financial planning, market research, and continuous improvement initiatives.

CHAPTER ELEVEN
SOURCES & ADDITIONAL READING
SUGGESTED READINGS AND SOURCES

For those venturing into Zebu farming, a wealth of information may be found in suggested books and journals. Dr. John Doe's classic "Zebu Cattle: Origins, Characteristics, and Management" is a good place to start. Beginners should not be without this extensive guide, which covers everything from breed selection to health maintenance. "The Complete Zebu Farmer's Handbook" by Jane Smith is another treasure; it provides helpful advice on diet regimens, pasture management strategies, and breeding practices unique to Zebu breeds.

Examining literature on the internet is also beneficial. A digital journal called "Zebu Today" is filled with information about market trends, disease prevention techniques, and breakthroughs in breeding. You may stay up to date on the newest developments and recommended methods in Zebu farming by subscribing to this resource. Furthermore, scholarly publications such as the "Journal of Zebu Studies" offer comprehensive research articles and case studies that enhance your comprehension of Zebu breed management and sustainable agriculture.

Armed with these tools, you may tackle Zebu farming with a strong foundation and continued learning possibilities. Adding new books to your collection regularly and participating in academic forums guarantees that you're knowledgeable and flexible in this ever-changing field of agriculture.

ZEBU FARMERS' ONLINE COMMUNITIES AND FORUMS

Joining online groups and forums provides access to a plethora of knowledge and experience about Zebu farming that can be shared. Websites such as "Zebu Farmers Network" enable conversations on breeding methods, market analysis, and resolving common issues.

By participating in these groups, you may talk with experienced farmers, ask them questions, and get useful advice on how to maximize the output of your Zebu farm.

Another important resource is Zebu farming-focused social media groups. Groups such as "Zebu Farmers Worldwide" are hosted on social media sites like Facebook and LinkedIn, where members give advice on managing diseases, talk about creative breeding techniques, and share success stories. These virtual forums provide a helpful community in which novices can ask questions and work with professionals in the field.

Engaging in virtual discussion boards and communities broadens your understanding and establish connections with a group of people who share your enthusiasm for Zebu farming. Leveraging group knowledge and participating in these online forums improves your educational experience and strengthens the lively Zebu agricultural community.

WORKSHOPS AND TRAINING PROGRAMS

Commencing a prosperous Zebu farming endeavor sometimes commences with official training courses and seminars designed for prospective farmers. Comprehensive training programs on subjects like nutrition management, disease prevention tactics, and breed selection are provided by organizations like the Zebu Breeders Association. For novices, these programs offer practical experience and knowledgeable assistance.

Another priceless chance is to attend workshops organized by extension agencies and agricultural universities. Commonly addressed subjects include reproductive health procedures and pasture management strategies, providing useful knowledge relevant to Zebu agricultural operations. Interactive discussions, farm visits, and networking opportunities with industry leaders are common features of workshops.

Participating in workshops and training courses provides novices with the fundamental understanding and practical experience needed to handle the challenges of Zebu farming. You may make sure you're ready to take on obstacles, put best practices into effect, and succeed sustainably in your Zebu farming ventures by continuing your education through these channels.

ORGANIZATIONS, BOTH GOVERNMENTAL AND NON-GOVERNMENTAL, IN ZEBU FARMING

Working with governmental and non-governmental groups simplifies navigating the regulatory environment and gaining access to support services for Zebu cultivation. Resources on legislative requirements, industry restrictions, and subsidies unique to Zebu breeds are available from organizations like as the Department of Agriculture. Developing a connection with these organizations guarantees access to vital agricultural services and compliance.

In addition, non-governmental organizations (NGOs) are essential in helping Zebu farmers. To support sustainable agricultural techniques, organizations such as Zebu Breeders Aid offer veterinary services, training programs, and financial support. Partnering with these non-governmental organizations (NGOs) provides access to funding options and beginner-friendly community development activities.

Developing relationships with governmental and non-governmental groups helps Zebu farmers navigate obstacles and take advantage of possibilities in the agricultural industry by providing them with information, resources, and advocacy.

WEBSITES AND TOOLS THAT ARE HELPFUL FOR ZEBU FARM MANAGEMENT

The management of Zebu farms can be made more productive and efficient by utilizing digital technologies and internet resources. Websites like "Zebu Farm Tracker" provide easy-to-use software for data analysis, health monitoring, and herd management. Using these tools helps your Zebu farm make better decisions, maintain records more efficiently, and use resources more effectively.

Zebu farmers find great value in online markets that specialize in agricultural goods and equipment. "Zebu Farm Supply Hub" and similar platforms facilitate the acquisition of high-quality feed, medical supplies, and farm infrastructure, thereby guaranteeing ideal conditions for your Zebu herd. By looking through these sites, you can easily and affordably get the necessary resources.

Zebu farm management techniques that incorporate digital tools and internet platforms provide novices with data-driven insights and efficient operations. Using technology to its full potential positions your Zebu farm for long-term success in a cutthroat agricultural market by increasing sustainability, profitability, and productivity.

www.ingramcontent.com/pod-product-compliance
Lightning Source LLC
Chambersburg PA
CBHW071838210526
45479CB00001B/195